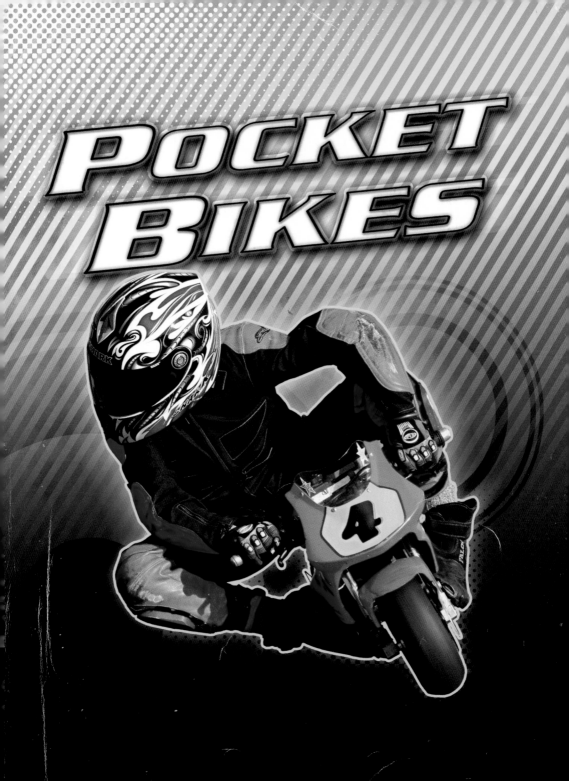

POCKET BIKES

BY THOMAS STREISSGUTH

TM

Are you ready to take it to the extreme?
Torque books thrust you into the action-packed
world of sports, vehicles, and adventure. These books
may include dirt, smoke, fire, and dangerous stunts.
WARNING: Read at your own risk.

Library of Congress Cataloging-in-Publication Data

Streissguth, Thomas, 1958–
  Pocket bikes / by Thomas Streissguth.
    p. cm. – (Torque–motorcycles)
  Summary: "Full color photography accompanies engaging information about Pocket Bikes.
The combination of high-interest subject matter and light text is intended for students in
grades 3 through 7"–Provided by publisher.
  Includes bibliographical references and index.
  ISBN–13: 978–1-60014–157–7 (hardcover : alk. paper)
  ISBN–10: 1–60014–157–9 (hardcover : alk. paper)
  1. Minibikes–Juvenile literature. I. Title.

TL443.S77 2008
629.227'5–dc22   2007040747

This edition first published in 2008 by Bellwether Media.

CONTENTS

WHAT IS A POCKET BIKE?

A pocket bike is part sport bike and part high-tech toy. Pocket bikes are wild-riding, knee-high motorcycles.

They're **mini bikes** built for adults. They can speed around a track at 50 miles (80 kilometers) per hour or faster. That may not sound fast. It feels extremely fast to a rider sitting only inches off the ground. Some people call pocket bikes "pocket rockets."

FAST FACT

POCKET BIKES ARE NOT LEGAL TO RIDE ON STREETS OR SIDEWALKS. RIDERS USE THEM ON CLOSED TRACKS OR OTHER PRIVATE PROPERTY. LAWBREAKERS RISK HAVING THEIR BIKES TAKEN AWAY BY THE POLICE.

Pocket bike racing started in Japan in the 1970s. People were tinkering with cheap, simple bikes made from spare parts. The Italians became interested in the 1980s. They began making higher-quality bikes. The Italians still make the best bikes in the sport. Pocket bike racing now attracts riders and die-hard fans from all over the world.

FEATURES

Pocket bike engines are small but effective. Most engines on basic starter bikes produce 3 to 4 **horsepower**. That's about the same as a lawn mower. The engines on high-end pocket bikes deliver up to 15 horsepower. That's still only about one-fourth the power of a **standard motorcycle**. Pocket bikes weigh around 50 pounds (22.7 kilograms). A small engine is enough to get a pocket bike moving fast.

Experienced riders claim that they can accelerate their pocket bikes from 0 to 49 miles (78.9 kilometers) per hour in five seconds.

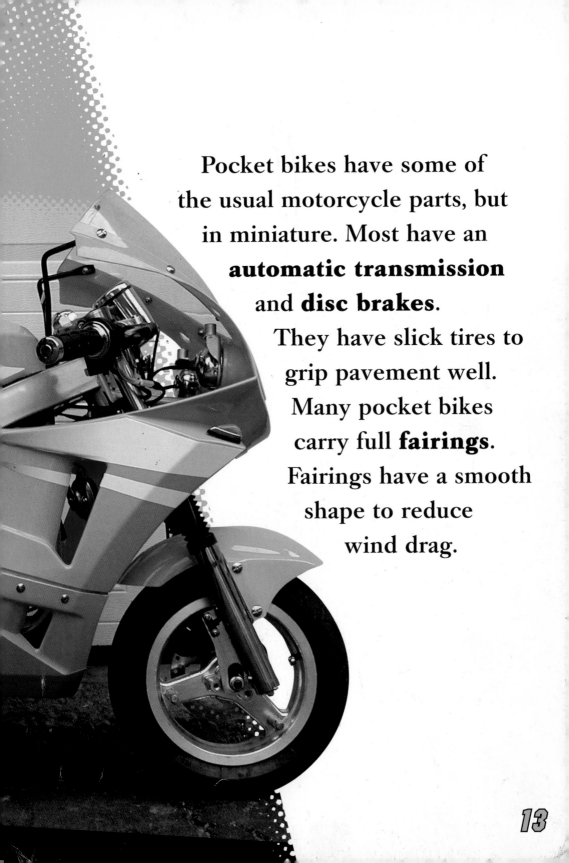

Pocket bikes have some of
the usual motorcycle parts, but
in miniature. Most have an
automatic transmission
and **disc brakes**.
They have slick tires to
grip pavement well.
Many pocket bikes
carry full **fairings**.
Fairings have a smooth
shape to reduce
wind drag.

FAST FACT

THE CURRENT RECORD SPEED ON A POCKET BIKE IS 78 MILES (125.5 KILOMETERS) PER HOUR. IT WAS SET BY A 5-FOOT-10-INCH (1.7-METER) BRITISH BIKER NAMED ALEC TAGUE.

Most pocket bikes have no **suspension system**. This helps keep the bikes lightweight. However, this also means that the rider has no cushion from the bumps of the road.

Pocket bike riders need good safety gear. Full-face helmets are essential. A wipeout on a pocket bike can be just as dangerous as one on a full-size motorcycle. Racers should also put on **sliders**. These protect knees from scraping the ground when rounding turns.

FAST FACT

POCKET BIKES COME IN A WIDE PRICE RANGE. THE CHEAPEST, MOST BASIC MODELS COST ABOUT $200. HIGHER-END MODELS CAN COST SEVERAL THOUSAND DOLLARS. $4,000 BUYS THE TOP OF THE LINE—A POCKET VERSION OF A DUCATI MOTORCYCLE.

POCKET BIKES
IN ACTION

Pocket bike racing
has become a craze
in certain places.
The "minimoto" **circuit** is
huge in Europe. The Swiss
Pocket Bike Championship,
created in 1996, has become
one of the largest pocket bike
championships in the world.
Japan and Australia also have
big races. The pocket bike
craze took off in the United
States in 2003.

Most pocket bike events are on oval tracks. An individual race is called a **heat**. The winners of the heats race in a final for the championship.

FAST FACT

VALENTINO ROSSI AND LORIS CAPIROSSI FROM ITALY AND NOBUATSU AOKI AND DAIJIRO KATO FROM JAPAN ARE ALL WORLD-CLASS PRO MOTORCYCLE RACERS WHO STARTED ON POCKET BIKES.

GLOSSARY

automatic transmission–a part of an engine that automatically changes gears according to the speed of a vehicle

circuit–a series of races run at different locations over the course of a racing season

disc brake–a mechanism that slows and stops the wheels with a flat, round metal disc

fairing–a fiberglass piece that extends from the frame of a motorcycle; fairings reduce wind drag.

heat–an individual pocket bike race

horsepower–a measure of the power of an engine

mini bike–a miniature version of a motorcycle; mini bikes made for adults are called pocket bikes.

sliders–kneepads worn by pocket bike racers over protective clothing

standard motorcycle–a basic street motorcycle without extra accessories

suspension system–a series of springs and shock absorbers that connect the body of a vehicle to its wheels

TO LEARN MORE

AT THE LIBRARY
Pupeza, Lori Kinstad. *Mini Bikes*. Edina, Minn.: Abdo, 1999.

Streissguth, Thomas. *Mini Bikes*. Minneapolis, Minn.: Bellwether, 2008.

ON THE WEB
Learning more about motorcycles is as easy as 1, 2, 3.

1. Go to www.factsurfer.com

2. Enter "motorcycles" into search box.

3. Click the "Surf" button and you will see a list of related web sites.

With factsurfer.com, finding more information is just a click away.

INDEX

The images in this book are reproduced through the courtesy of:
Henk Bentlage, front cover, p. 8; Andrea Leone, pp. 5, 15, 21; Roslina
binti Yusoff, pp. 6-7, 9, 19, 20; Clive Mason/Getty Images, pp. 11, 14, 17;
Cindy Lynn Dockrill, pp. 12-13; Steve Bonini/Getty Images, p. 16.